MW00611374

Your Steps towards Greatness

Table of Contents

Introduction

"The way of success is the way of continuous pursuit of knowledge."- Napoleon Hill

Use these fact sheets to explore the 17 Principles while focusing on your favorite ideas. Feel free to copy them into your smartphone or use notecards.

If you need support, reach out to a teacher, mentor, or someone you can trust to help you understand the concepts carefully. Finally, have fun, as you choose what will help you best now.

Of course, you can write your own insight and return to the book whenever you want to check your progress thus far. Enjoy!

Step 1

Your Purpose

Begin with a Burning Desire

Develop a DEFINITE PURPOSE

Fact Sheet 1A   How Purpose Affects Action

Right now, make up in your mind exactly what you desire.

Fix your imagination on your outstanding major goal in life.

Next, determine exactly what you will give in return.

Then, assess what is necessary to make it a reality.

After that, set a specific date for attaining this goal.

Next, follow your desire with a clear definite plan for carrying out your purpose.

Last, put your plan into action immediately.

Fact Sheet 1B   **Your Burning Desire**

- Clearly define your plan for achievement.

- Write your outstanding major goal (or burning desire) in detail including, when you want it, and what you intend to give in exchange for realizing it.

  - Make sure your plan is flexible and allows for adjustments.

  - Your outstanding major goal, known as your Burning Desire, should not change. Yet your plan for achieving it may change many times.

- Each day when you awaken and before you sleep read what you wrote aloud. As you read—see, feel, and imagine living out your major objective.

- On a regular basis, evaluate yourself to determine whether you are staying on the path (without deviating too much) for your objective.

- Finally, ensure your success by freely using your time to study, think, and plan regarding how you can achieve your outstanding major goal in life.

Quote to remember:

Successful people move upon their own initiative. Yet often they know where they are going before they begin.

Step 2

Your Inner Circle

Create a Tight Group that Has Your Back

Establish a MASTERMIND ALLIANCE

Fact Sheet 2: Your Inner Circle (Mastermind)

Your inner circle or Mastermind Alliance is the "axis" or "hub" where your path to succeed rests.

When working with others, know that no one truly succeeds alone. It takes the efforts of others to aid you in your goals.

Remember:

- Your inner circle is a Mastermind Alliance where two or more people harmonize efforts to achieve a significant goal.
- The good news is that you can have several alliances, each with its own goal.

Examples of Alliances include:

- You and brother work in sync to do the chores (he cuts the grass; you clean the kitchen & bathroom) after school on Thursdays. Both of you meet the family goal of housework.
- You and your best friend play soccer and have a burning desire to make the team.
- You and a couple of your close friends work in the afterschool tutoring program at least 1 hour a week to win the school spirit award.

Step 3
Your Personality

Become who you need to succeed

Assemble an ATTRACTIVE PERSONALITY

Fact Sheet 3 Cultivate Your
Pleasing Personality

Creating a winning personality is not impossible.

From the list below, identify 2 – 3 qualities that you can embrace now as you develop a personality that is pleasant and draws others.

Don't feel like you have to improve everything at once. **Just start where you are.**

Positivity**	Self-Awareness
Flexibility	Persuasiveness
Authenticity	Multitalented
Decisiveness	Compassionate
Respect	Thoughtfulness
Diplomacy	Entertaining
Well-Spoken	Disciplined
Inviting & Friendly	Patience
Open-Mindedness	Modesty
Honesty	Focused
Funny	Classy
Full of Faith	Flair
Principled	Competitiveness
Precision	Confidence
Consideration	Charismatic

**Note: You will learn more about a positive mental attitude in Step 7: Your Attitude—Positivity Sees Opportunity.

Step 4

Your Confidence

Believe by Doing

Use APPLIED FAITH

Fact Sheet 4A   Your Confidence & Faith

The more you do what you believe, the more your confidence grows.

Fear

Doubt

Faith

Fear is like a red light. It stops you from moving forward in your goals. Fear is faith in reverse. Doubt is like a yellow light. It slows you down, and you can only proceed with caution. Faith is like a green light. You move forward free and unhindered. Simply put, applied faith is believing by doing.

Applied Faith is a quality like self-confidence. It goes beyond individual ability & taps into an assurance that what you desire will happen regardless of circumstances or conditions opposing you.

Fact Sheet 4B   Faith as a Divine Quality

Faith provides you with insight & **access** to universal power beyond your normal capabilities.

It is considered a "divine" quality throughout the world.

<u>**Remember**</u>:
- Faith without action steps is pointless & empty.
- Faith grows through intense, persistent action.
- Applied Faith is the art of believing by doing.
- Fear is faith in reverse gear.
- Faith leads to direct communication with Infinite Intelligence.

Fact Sheet 4C   Affirmations

Faith says, "Yes!" to desires & commands what you want to appear. Faith recognizes limitless paths to your desires.

What you believe about yourself and the words you use shape your reality.

Affirmations place you into a state of belief where you repeatedly say and act on your desires with full confidence.

To build your faith, you must speak your desires with intense emotion and passion.

<u>Consider saying your affirmations at least twice a day.</u>
Here are a few suggestions to use:

Affirmations:
* I love me—mind, body, & soul.
* I believe; therefore, all things are possible for me.
* I spend my money wisely and maturely.
* Setbacks & defeat do not rule me. I never give up on my dreams.
* I find ways to make my dreams a reality. I will find a way to win.

<u>Step 5</u>

Your Work Ethic

Grind or Be Left in the Dust

Go the EXTRA MILE

Fact Sheet 5 — Work Ethic & Pay

To summarize, use this formula

Q1 +	Q2 +	MA =	C
The Quality of service given	The Quantity of service provided	Your Mental Attitude when you do it [1]	Your Compensation

Your Compensation is not only your reward in the world.

It is the degree of gratitude you receive from others for your service.

REASONS TO GIVE MORE & BETTER SERVICE

- You feel better about yourself & strengthen your character.
- You receive praise & pay far beyond what you give in service.
  - a. It may come from the person you serve.
  - b. It may come from others who see & want you on their team or in their organization.
- You develop courage, confidence & personal initiative.
- You become more enthusiastic about serving.
- You may discover your calling in the world making it easier to gain positions you want in society.

---

[1] Please note: The best "mental attitude" is a Positive Mental Attitude. You will learn more about this in Step 7.

<u>Step 6</u>

Your Ambition

Act Now. Procrastination Kills.

Create PERSONAL INITIATIVE

Fact Sheet 6 Develop Your Personal Initiative

Personal initiative is your inner power that _drives_ action.

The power to inspire & complete your goals begins with your personal initiative.

Personal initiative fuels fire for major & minor goals.

People with personal initiative see favorable opportunities and make the most of them.

Those with personal initiative possess an insatiable thirst for new ways to reach goals.

Quote to remember:

Ready or not, here I come! With strength I chase my goals, no matter what life or circumstances may bring!

Step 7

Your Attitude

Positivity Sees Opportunity

Build a POSITIVE MENTAL ATTITUDE

Fact Sheet 7A   Ways to Develop a Positive Mental Attitude

A Positive Mental Attitude (aka PMA) means that you are self-confident & see opportunity—not limitations. So go after it! Just don't break laws or hurt others.

Through willpower, you create a PMA based upon your motive & ability to adapt.

To develop a PMA, understand the Golden Rule—treat others the way you want to be treated.

Apply the Golden Rule. Be considerate & sensitive to other's reactions.

Next, monitor your own responses. Control your behaviors & your reactions to your environment.

Believe strongly that your burning ambition can be achieved.

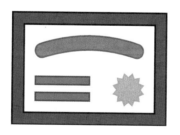

Finally, develop right habits of thought & action that contribute to success day by day.

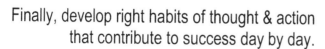

Fact Sheet 7B   Results of a Positive Mental Attitude

A <u>Positive Mental Attitude</u> describes a person with right, honest, and constructive thoughts most of the time. Their response to any situation respects the rights of others and the environment around them.

You become more friendly with a positive mental attitude. It compels you to actively pursue your driving desire in life. A PMA fuels enthusiasm, self-control and cooperation with others while allowing your imagination to flourish.

Here are some outcomes of the Positive Mental Attitude:

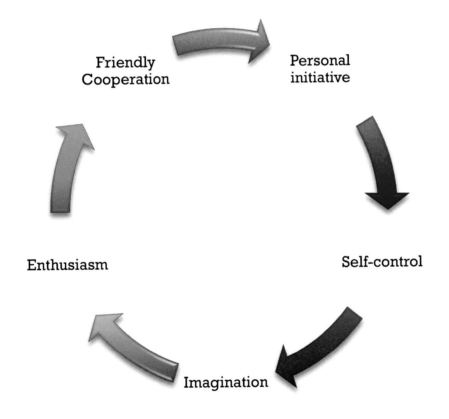

Friendly
Cooperation

Personal
initiative

Enthusiasm

Self-control

Imagination

Step 8

Your Enthusiasm

Let Your Passion Flow Through Channels

Control Your ENTHUSIASM

Fact Sheet 8A How Enthusiasm Flows

Connect to a water source

Identify an Aquifer

Prime the Pump

Allow Enthusiasm to be Channeled

Open Valve for Flow

Water flows freely uninterrupted

Fact Sheet 8B   *Channel Enthusiasm*

 Channeling Your Enthusiasm Effectively

1. Connect to a water source. Link your enthusiasm to something deeper. This can be a driving desire, concern for others, or pursuit of fame or creative expression.

Your connection is like drawing water from an aquifer.

2. Prime the Pump. Allow inspiration to focus your energy and push enthusiasm out. It is focused energy.

This is like pressurized water coming out of the pump.

3. Open the Valve for Flow. Your open-mindedness and passion about your goals allows you to speak freely & naturally from your thoughts, feelings, & emotions.

Let enthusiasm flow freely like water. Allow it to continually refresh you.

<u>Step 9</u>

Your Discipline

Ignore the Noise & Go After It

Enforce SELF-DISCIPLINE

Fact Sheet 9   **Focus! Discipline at its Best**

Self-Discipline enables you to develop control over yourself. Keep in mind that both successes and failures are the results of your habits.

It begins with mastery
of your thoughts.

We are creatures of
habit because we are a
mind with a body.

The good news is that
we can change our
habits.

Quote to remember:

Channel your thoughts to control your emotions. Your willpower determines your destiny.

<u>Step 10</u>

Your Thoughts

Separate Truth from Rumors & Lies

THINK ACCURATELY

Fact Sheet 10A   *Searching for Truth*

Learn more about Inductive & Deductive Reasoning

"Man can alter his life by altering his thinking." --William James

Inductive reasoning is persuading others to believe you through stories and examples. It accepts assumptions or unknown facts.

Deductive reasoning traces logic like breadcrumbs to the source. It accepts known facts or what we believe to be facts.

To be an accurate thinker, you must:

1. Separate facts from rumor or fiction.

2. Separate facts into two categories, important & unimportant.

Remember: "Truth will always be truth, regardless of lack of understanding, disbelief, or ignorance." --W. Clement Stone

Fact Sheet 10B

Logic v. Application
Deductive v. Inductive

Are you running out of time to explain yourself? Do you need to be more direct?

The strength of Deductive Reasoning lies in presenting information concisely. It focuses on quick solutions to problems.

✓ *Its goal is to build rational arguments.*

Do you need a story to explain a complex idea?

Do you need to go over this idea multiple times to ensure people understand you?

The strength of Inductive Reasoning lies in repeating information regularly to build impact on what is possible.

✓ *It uses the imagination to fuel subconscious problem-solving.*

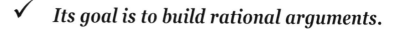

Do you need brevity or to be direct?	It's all about the <u>Logic</u>	**Use Deductive Reasoning**	Its strength lies in presenting information concisely as it focuses on discovering solutions to problems.
Do you need repetition?	It's all about the <u>Application</u>	**Use Inductive Reasoning**	Its strength lies in repeating information regularly as it impacts the subconscious.

Use <u>both</u> to your advantage.

Step 11

Your Focus

Lock In On What's Important

Control YOUR ATTENTION

Fact Sheet 11

Direct Your Aim

Napoleon Hill once said, "You have, in your own power, in your mind, the capacity to acquire whatever you want."

Controlled attention is <u>organized mind power</u>.

- Controlled attention coordinates every part of the mind & directs its combined power towards a burning desire.
- Success, in higher brackets of achievement, is impossible without focus. Learn to focus your thoughts and mental energy for definite ends.
  - Your mind never rests and always seeks goals—positive or negative.
  - What you put in, comes out, in your day-to-day life. Choose your thoughts wisely.

<u>Controlled attention flows from self-discipline.</u>

Step 12

Your Team

Link Up with Others to Win Big

Inspire TEAMWORK

Fact Sheet 12A   Teamwork at its Best

Teamwork exists when people coordinate their efforts & support one another to achieve a specific objective.

When the spirit of teamwork is willing, upbeat, & voluntary, it leads to gaining great & lasting power. Teamwork creates success in your home, school, community, government, business & personal life.

Remember:

- Teamwork builds dreams for you personally & for others.
- Teamwork provides unlimited opportunity for all involved.
- Cooperation through teamwork shares the best part of what you have with others.

Quote to Remember:

Teamwork is supporting others to achieve a common goal. For each team player, what you share multiplies the team's power. The opposite is also true.

Fact Sheet 12B *Defining Characteristics between Your Team & Your Inner Circle*[2]

Your Team (Teamwork)	vs.	Your Inner Circle (Mastermind)
2+ people working together to accomplish a goal		2+ people working on a shared burning desire or obsession
Participation may be willing or forced		Composed of willing participants
Leaders may need to "Go the Extra Mile" to get cooperation from members		Members are deeply bonded and work together collaboratively
Members are selected based on roles, talents, or abilities		Each member fulfills a unique role & values each other's contributions
Compensation is often standardized (e.g., pay, grades, etc.)		Compensation is unique to the desires of each member
Work hours are often standardized		Efforts are not limited to traditional work hours
Meet as needed		Meet 1+ times weekly
Motivated primarily by compensation		Motivated primarily by the burning desire
Information is compartmentalized on a "as-needed" basis		All information is shared equally among all members
Have "limited" to "no role" in decision-making on the overall project		Everyone must agree prior to taking action

---

[2] Please note: Your team is often larger than your inner circle. Your inner circle is closer knit. The chart makes this clear. If you are missing any parts of the components of your inner circle, known as a "Mastermind" then most likely you have a team.

<u>Step 13</u>

Your Resilience

Failure & Loss Teach. . .

If You Let Them

Learn from ADVERSITY AND DEFEAT

Fact Sheet 13: Find the Seed (or Lesson) in Adversity & Defeat

Every disappointment, every defeat, & every adversity carry within it the seed of an equivalent or greater value.

How can you discover this seed or lesson?

You can find it by considering each setback in a different light.

- View each defeat as a steppingstone, not as a stumbling block.
- Temporary failure is Nature's way of teaching us resilience and revealing what you need to work on.

Remember:

- People with a positive mental attitude typically react to defeat with determination and an unwillingness to accept it as the end.
- A person with a negative mental attitude reacts to defeat with hopelessness, self-pity, & despair.
- Many who attain high level victories usually experience some significant defeat or failure before reaching success.

Quote to Remember:

During times of disappointment, defeat, and challenge, I chose to refocus my mind. I will live my beliefs moment by moment and find the seed (or lesson) that I need to learn from the experience.

Step 14

Your Imagination

Dream Big but Plan Bigger.

Cultivate CREATIVE VISION

Fact Sheet 14A *Imagination in Action*

Your Cell phone call = Your Burning Desire
Your burning desire is like making a cell phone call into the realm of possibility.

Relays to Broadcast Tower = Applied Faith
When you act on what you believe, your applied faith 'thoughtcasts' your actions to others & your subconscious mind.

Orbital Satellite Dish = Subconscious Mind

If you focus on your burning desire regularly, your subconscious mind recognizes your unflinching efforts & reveals ways to achieve it.

On Ground Receiving Dish = Creative Vison
Your creative imagination takes these ideas from the subconscious & gives you fresh ideas or new twists on old ideas to work these visions practically & passionately.

You Relay Plans to Your Inner Circle
Sharing your plans with the inner circle motivates them as well. Therefore, your imagination positively influences others committed to helping you achieve your goal.

Fact Sheet 14B *The World of Imagination*

It creates, visualizes & analyzes.	It foresees & generates ideas.	It compares & chooses.

You can find inspiration from:

Music

Photos

Travel

Remember:
Whatever you can visualize in your mind

becomes rocket fuel

for your creative efforts.

Step 15

Your Health

What You Put In—Shows Out

Maintain SOUND HEALTH

Fact Sheet 15A Physical & Mental Health

You are a mind with a body.

The wise man should consider that health is the greatest of human blessings. Let food be your medicine. —Hippocrates

In the same way your brain regulates your body, recognize that sound physical health often requires positivity to promote full awareness of good health.

You should:

- **Establish good, well-balanced health habits for school, play, rest, work, diet, & study.**
- **Practice wellness. Focus on maintaining good health instead of just avoiding illness or disease.**

Remember: What your mind focuses upon directs where your energy is spent —whether physical or mental.

Fact Sheet 15B *Being Well-Balanced*

Use self-discipline to your advantage.

Practice mindfulness & keep your mind free of negative thoughts & influences.

To become well-balanced in health, remember:

<u>Always</u>:

FOLLOW SCHOOL		**WITH PLAY**	
Follow Mental effort		With Physical effort	
Follow Seriousness		With Humor	

"Your health is what you make of it. Everything you do and think either adds to the vitality, energy and spirit you possess or takes away from it." –Ann Wigmore

40

Step 16

Your Time & Money

Exchange These for What You Need

Budget your TIME AND MONEY

Fact Sheet 16 **Personal Inventory for Time & Money**

Plan your work and work your plan. —Napoleon Hill

Learn how your time & money practices impact your goals. **Find a clear balance between time & resources.**

Remember:

- If you take personal inventory, chances are that you will find areas that need improvement.
- Success doesn't require you to know everything in the world. Instead, commit to use the knowledge you have. This includes:
    a. The knowledge of time.
    b. The understanding of money.

<u>Step 17</u>

Your Habits

What You Do Fuels Who You Become

Use COSMIC HABITFORCE

Fact Sheet 17   Your Habits & the Environment

We are shaped & ruled by 'habitcraft'.

A large part of where we are is based on our established habits, thoughts, & deeds.

Create thought habits by repeating desired ideas & behaviors until *Natural Law* takes over the new habits & makes them stable until you consciously rearrange them.

In short, we have many habits.

- Some are good, while undesirable ones, may need changing.
- Each of us must think in a way to develop strong good habits, as well as neutralize or change destructive habits, through calculated thoughts & actions.

Remember:

- Replace a negative habit with a stronger positive habit. Develop good habits today in harmony with your ability to achieve an outstanding major purpose.

Quote to remember:

Sow an act & you reap a habit.
Sow a habit & you reap a character.
Sow a character & you reap a destiny.

Conclusion

Thank you for reviewing this guide.
We hope it has been helpful.
We conclude by asking you one question:

Q: What did you learn and how will you apply it to your life?

Whatever the mind can conceive & believe, it can achieve.   - Napoleon Hill

We wish you the best as you climb your steps of success!

Made in the USA
Columbia, SC
07 April 2022

58655515R00029